Think Twice

The Art of Seeing Through Nonsense in a
World Full of It

Kalembwe Mwape

Think Twice

Table of Contents

Introduction: The Happiness Hustlers 2

Chapter 1: The Ten-Step Trap 11

Chapter 2: The Self-Help Industrial Complex......22

Chapter 3: The Anatomy of a Charlatan...............37

Chapter 4: The Psychology of Sucker-Proneness..53

Chapter 5: The Greatest Hits of BS Advice 62

Chapter 6: The Weight Loss Wasteland 74

Chapter 7: The Get-Rich-Quick Cemetery..........83

Chapter 8: The Relationship Racket....................96

Chapter 9: Breaking Free from the BS 104

Chapter 10: The Uncomfortable Truth 116

Appendix A: The BS Bingo Card.......................134

Appendix B: The Wall of Shame 141

About Author...148

Credits 149

Copyright 150

Introduction: The Happiness Hustlers

Let's start with a confession: I'm writing this book because I've been a sucker. Multiple times. I've bought the courses, downloaded the PDFs, and nodded along to YouTube videos promising to transform my life in the time it takes to microwave a burrito. If you're reading this, chances are you have too. Don't worry – this isn't where I tell you I've discovered the *real* secret to happiness. (Though if I were a proper charlatan, I'd definitely say that.)

The Rise of the Five-Step Solution Factory

Let's start with the golden rule of modern snake oil: if it sounds too good to be true, someone is probably making money off it. Enter the world of happiness hustlers—those smiling, well-dressed peddlers of life's easy answers. They sell you solutions in shiny packages: five steps, ten rules, seven habits, one weird trick. And the best part? Their advice always seems to hit that sweet spot between obvious and ground-breaking.

You're desperate for clarity, and they're ready to deliver it—for the price of a book, a course, or, if you're really lucky, a three-day seminar that includes free snacks. They know you're tired, overwhelmed, and secretly hoping that someone has already figured out life and distilled it into a neat little checklist. And boy, do they have checklists for you.

The self-help industrial complex has mastered the art of turning every human struggle into a numbered list that would fit on a Pinterest board. It's like they've discovered some cosmic law that says all of life's problems can be solved in ten steps or fewer. Anything more would hurt sales; anything less wouldn't justify the $297 price tag.

But here's the catch: the checklist is never for their benefit. It's for yours—at least, that's what they claim. In reality, it's the oldest con in the book: they sell the fantasy, not the reality. Because reality, let's face it, is messy, complicated, and utterly resistant to bullet points.

Why We're All Desperate for Quick Fixes

Let's not pretend we're above it. We've all been there—scrolling through social media at 2 a.m., watching some "guru" explain how waking up at 4:30 a.m. changed their life. Suddenly, you're convinced that your main problem isn't your crushing debt, your toxic job, or the fact that you're subsisting on instant noodles. No, your problem is that you're not drinking green juice while journaling your gratitude affirmations.

Here's the uncomfortable truth: we're not stupid. We're tired. We're overwhelmed. We're living in a world where everything moves at the speed of Wi-Fi, and we're still operating on human hardware that evolved to run from tigers and gather berries. When someone comes along and says, "Hey, I can fix your entire life in less time than it takes to binge-watch a season of your favourite show," it's not just appealing – it feels like survival.

The real genius of the modern snake oil salesman isn't that they're particularly convincing. It's that they've perfectly timed their pitch to catch us at our most vulnerable moments:

Late at night when we can't sleep because we're worried about money? Here's a forex trading course that "literally prints cash."

Scrolling through Instagram feeling bad about our bodies? Here's a miracle diet that lets you eat whatever you want (as long as whatever you want is air and disappointment).

Feeling stuck in your career? Here's a "fool-proof" system to become a millionaire entrepreneur by next Tuesday.

It's tempting to believe there's a shortcut, isn't it? A quick fix to untangle the Gordian knot of modern existence. We want to believe that success, happiness, and fulfilment are just a matter of following the right recipe. And if that recipe involves ten easy steps, even better. Double points if there's a numbered list somewhere in the mix.

The truth is, we're wired to seek patterns, even when none exist. That's why we fall for these things. We see a smiling author holding a book called How to Win at Life Without Even Trying, and we think, "Maybe this time it's different." Spoiler: it's never different.

A Brief History of Getting Duped (And Why We Keep Coming Back for More)

Humans have been falling for quick fixes since the first caveperson tried to sell their neighbour a rock guaranteed to keep tigers away. (Spoiler: The rock worked great on imaginary tigers.) But something changed with the advent of social media and the democratization of influence. Suddenly, anyone with good lighting and the ability to speak in absolutes could become a "thought leader."

Snake oil salesmen aren't new. They've just upgraded their wardrobes and swapped wagons for Instagram accounts. The original snake oil, for the record, was literal: 19th-century con artists sold fake cures made of mineral oil and spices, claiming it could cure everything from arthritis to baldness. Today, instead of peddling dubious elixirs, modern hustlers peddle dubious ideas.

The self-help industry is the great-grandchild of this tradition, with roots in everything from Victorian etiquette manuals to the New Thought movement of the early 20th century. Back then, the idea was that thinking good thoughts could manifest good outcomes—essentially the spiritual ancestor of "manifesting" your dreams today.

We keep falling for it because hope sells. It always has. The hope that this time, this book, this method, this guru will finally have the answer. And when it inevitably doesn't, we blame ourselves, not the system. We think, "Maybe I didn't follow the steps correctly. Maybe I need to try harder." And so, the cycle continues.

It's not just that we fall for it once – we fall for it over and over, like goldfish with credit cards, each time convinced that *this* is the real deal. Why? Because hope is addictive, and admitting that there are no easy answers feels like giving up.

But here's the hard truth: there is no "secret." No universal formula. No magic bullet. And the sooner we accept that, the sooner we can stop wasting time on charlatans and start figuring out what actually works—for us, as individuals, in our messy, unique lives.

What This Book Is (And Isn't)

This isn't another self-help book. It's a self-defence manual for your brain. We're going to explore the mechanics of how we get duped, why even smart people fall for obvious scams, and how to spot the red flags before they cost you your money, time, and dignity.

Will this book solve all your problems? Absolutely not. Will it give you a numbered list of steps to happiness? Only if you're not paying attention. What it will do is help you develop a finely-tuned BS detector and save you from buying another course that promises to teach you how to make six figures while sleeping.

Fair warning: If you're looking for comfortable lies and easy answers, you might want to close this book now. There are plenty of Instagram coaches waiting to sell you those. But if you're ready to understand why we're so susceptible to snake oil and how to break free from the cycle of quick-fix addiction, stick around. It's going to be an uncomfortable ride, but at least it'll be honest.

And hey, if nothing else, you'll save enough money on useless courses to afford a really nice dinner. Sometimes that's better than a transformation anyway.

Chapter 1: The Ten-Step Trap

Ever notice how every life-changing solution comes in exactly ten steps? Not nine. Not eleven. Ten. It's like the self-help industry discovered the metric system but stopped at their fingers. If aliens studied our species through Instagram captions and Medium articles, they'd assume humans were physically incapable of processing any other number of steps.

The Magic of Round Numbers

There's something almost mystical about how charlatans pick their numbers. Three steps? Too short — people won't feel like they're getting their money's worth. Fifteen steps? Whoa there, professor, we're trying to fix lives here, not write a dissertation. But ten? Ten is the Goldilocks of BS. It's long enough to seem comprehensive but short enough to fit on an infographic that your aunt will share on Facebook.

Want to lose weight? Ten steps. Find love? Ten steps. Build a billion-dollar business? Ten steps. It's as if life itself has been waiting patiently to align with our decimal system, just so self-help authors can crank out yet another "life-changing" guide.

The truth is, round numbers are comforting. They feel complete. Nobody writes a book called Eleven and a Half Rules for Better Relationships because odd numbers and fractions don't sell. Ten feels authoritative, like someone has done the math and distilled the chaos of existence into an orderly, digestible list. But let's be real: life is messy, complex, and full of nuance. The idea that every problem can be reduced to a neat, round-numbered formula is absurd on its face.

Why Every Problem Apparently Has Exactly Ten Solutions

Here's a little secret: the "ten steps" aren't there to help you—they're there to sell you. Publishers know that you're more likely to buy a book that promises clarity and structure. It doesn't matter if the advice is garbage. If it's wrapped in the reassuring framework of ten steps, you'll at least give it a glance.

Here's a fun game: Pick any problem. Literally any problem. Now Google it with "10 steps" in front of it. I guarantee someone has written a "definitive" ten-step solution for it. Here are some real examples I found:

* "10 Steps to Training Your Pet Rock"

* "10 Steps to Becoming a Morning Person (Even If You're Literally Nocturnal)"

* "10 Steps to Understanding Why You Need These 10 Steps"

The beautiful irony is that the more complex the problem, the more likely you are to find it reduced to ten steps. Relationship falling apart after 20 years? Ten steps. Want to become a billionaire? Ten steps. Trying to find the meaning of life? You better believe that's ten steps.

The ten-step trap is marketing genius. It preys on our cognitive biases, particularly our desire for simplicity and our tendency to trust authoritative-sounding frameworks. When we see a list, we assume it's been thought through, that someone with expertise carefully curated these steps just for us. In reality, most of these lists are arbitrary, cobbled together to hit a word count and justify the price tag.

The Psychology of "Easy" Solutions

Let's talk about why we fall for these lists in the first place. It's not just that they're neatly packaged—it's that they offer the illusion of control. When life feels overwhelming, the idea of following ten simple steps to fix everything is intoxicating. Our brains are basically lazy pattern-matching machines running on coffee and anxiety. When we see something broken down into steps, two things happen:

1. We feel relief: "Finally! Someone has organized this chaos!"

2. We feel hope: "I can do ten things! I do at least ten things before lunch!"

The problem is that real solutions rarely come in neat, numbered packages. Life is messy. Progress is messy. Success is messy. But "Ten Steps to Embracing the Chaotic, Non-

Linear Nature of Personal Growth and Accept That There Are No Easy Answers" doesn't sell as well as "Ten Steps to Your Best Life NOW!"

Think about it: you're struggling with your career, your relationships, and your mental health. Along comes a book titled Ten Steps to Total Life Mastery, and suddenly, you're hooked. It doesn't matter that the advice is generic, impractical, or downright harmful. What matters is that it feels actionable.

Of course, the problem with easy solutions is that they're rarely solutions at all. Real change is hard, messy, and rarely linear. But nobody wants to hear that. So instead, we cling to these lists like drowning people clutching at straws, hoping against hope that this time, the steps will work.

Case Study: How I Wrote This Chapter in Three Simple Steps (Spoiler: I Didn't)

If this book were a self-help scam, I'd end this chapter with my own ten-step formula for avoiding ten-step formulas. Something like:

1. Identify the BS.
2. Reject the BS.
3. Profit.

But let's not kid ourselves. Writing this chapter wasn't a tidy, linear process. It involved caffeine-fuelled brainstorming sessions, half-finished drafts, and several moments of existential dread. Real life doesn't fit into neat little boxes, and neither does real work.

And yet, if I slapped those three steps on the back of a book cover, you'd probably find it tempting. That's the trap. We want solutions to be simple because complexity is scary. But the moment we fall for simplicity at the expense of truth, we're no better than the suckers buying snake oil.

The Step-Step Fallacy

Here's what the step-pushers don't want you to realize: breaking something into steps doesn't make it easier — it just makes it look easier. It's like those "simple" IKEA instructions that show four cheerful drawings of someone assembling a bookcase, conveniently leaving out the part where you're on the floor at 2 AM, surrounded by mysterious extra screws, questioning every life decision that led you to this moment.

Real talk: Some things don't need steps. Some things need time, patience, practice, failure, and more failure. But "Ten Steps to Accepting That Some Things Just Take Time and There Are No Shortcuts" doesn't make for a very catchy TED Talk.

Breaking Free from Step Addiction

The first step to breaking free from the ten-step trap is... just kidding. I'm not going to give you steps for breaking free from steps. That's like hosting an Alcoholics Anonymous meeting in a bar.

Instead, try this: The next time you see something broken down into exactly ten steps, ask yourself:

* Why ten?

* What's being left out?

* What makes this person qualified to reduce this complex issue to ten bullet points?

* Am I being sold hope in a numbered list?

Remember: Real solutions rarely come in perfectly packaged steps. They come with mess, uncertainty, and usually a few metaphorical (or literal) tears. And that's okay. Actually, that's normal.

Conclusion: The Real Cost of the Ten-Step Trap

The ten-step trap isn't just annoying—it's dangerous. It perpetuates the myth that life's problems can be solved quickly, easily, and universally. It sets us up for disappointment, self-blame, and endless cycles of buying more books, courses, and programs in the hope that this one will finally work.

But here's the truth: there are no universal steps, no magic formulas, no shortcuts. And the sooner we stop looking for them, the sooner we can start doing the hard, messy work of figuring out what actually works for us.

So, the next time someone promises you ten steps to success, ask yourself: are they selling you a solution, or are they just selling you?

In the next chapter, we'll dive into the billion-dollar industry built around selling you steps you don't need to solve problems they didn't invent. Spoiler alert: It's going to make you mad. Good. You should be.

Chapter 2: The Self-Help Industrial Complex

Welcome to the billion-dollar business of making you feel terrible about yourself and then selling you the cure. It's like a protection racket for your self-esteem: "Nice confidence you got there. Shame if something happened to it. But hey, for just twelve payments of $99.99..."

The Billion-Dollar BS Business

Let's start with some numbers: the self-help industry is worth over $10 billion annually. That's billion with a "B." And what do we get for all that money? A shiny graveyard of books, courses, and motivational calendars that didn't actually help. That's right – we're spending billions on books, courses, and seminars that basically tell us to drink water and go to bed earlier. If someone had pitched this business model a century ago, they'd have been laughed out of the room:

"So, what's your business plan?"

"I'm going to tell people to breathe deeply and journal."

"And they'll pay you for this?"

"No, they'll pay me BILLIONS for this."

Here's the beautiful irony: most of these "life-changing" products are created by people who made their money by... teaching others how to make money. It's like a pyramid scheme, but with more inspirational quotes.

Self-help is the perfect con. First, it convinces you that you're broken—just enough to buy their product but not so much that you lose hope. Then, it sells you the dream of a better you. Finally, when their advice inevitably fails, they whisper, "Maybe you didn't try hard enough," and point you to their next offering. Rinse and repeat.

But here's the real kicker: the people at the top of this pyramid aren't following their own advice. You think the author of 5 AM Morning Routines for Success is waking up at dawn to meditate and do yoga? Please. They're too busy cashing checks and laughing at your naïveté.

Inside the "Expert" Factory

So, who are these self-help "experts," anyway? Spoiler: most of them aren't experts. They're marketers. They're performers. They're people who figured out that confidence and charisma can sell anything, even if the product is hot air.

Becoming a self-help guru is shockingly easy.

Step one: create a personal origin story. Ideally, it involves some kind of dramatic failure followed by an equally dramatic comeback. "I was homeless, broke, and surviving on instant ramen—until I discovered [insert vague concept here]. Now I'm a millionaire, and you can be too!"

Step two: slap a catchy title on a book or course. Something like Unleash Your Inner Alpha or Manifest Your Dream Life. Bonus points if it includes words like "secret," "ultimate," or "hack."

Step three: get a professional headshot of yourself looking thoughtful but approachable. You're selling a lifestyle, not just advice, and people need to believe they can be as annoyingly successful as you appear to be.

Step four: go viral. Post inspirational quotes on Instagram. Start a podcast. Pay for ads. Suddenly, you're an "authority" on personal growth, even if your qualifications are non-existent.

The barrier to entry in the expert industry is so low it's practically a tripping hazard. You don't need credentials, experience, or even basic grammar skills. All you need is confidence, a ring light, and the ability to say "paradigm shift" with a straight face.

The Certification Racket

Sure, there are "certifications" available. For a modest fee (usually around the price of a used car), you too can become a certified master life coach in just two weekends! Because apparently, that's all it takes to understand the complexities of human psychology and personal development. Freud spent years developing his theories, but Karen from Instagram figured it all out during a retreat in Bali.

Instagram Gurus and Their Perfect Morning Routines

You've seen them on Instagram: the gurus with their pristine kitchens, perfect lighting, and effortlessly styled loungewear. They wake up at 4 a.m., drink a kale smoothie, meditate for 30 minutes, and write in their gratitude journals—all before tackling their highly curated, dream-like to-do list. Their feed is a carefully curated collection of:

* Motivational quotes they definitely didn't write

* Photos of their "humble" workspace (featuring a $5,000 chair)

* Their "simple" morning routine that somehow takes 6 hours

* Screenshots of their "passive income" (taken during the 3 minutes it was actually impressive)

Let's talk about these morning routines, because they're my favourite form of aspirational fiction. According to these gurus, here's what you should do before 6 AM:

- Meditate for an hour
- Journal for an hour
- Work out for two hours
- Read three books
- Make a green smoothie that costs $47 in ingredients
- Manifest abundance
- Solve world hunger
- Learn three languages
- Build a rocket ship

And if you're not doing all of this? Well, clearly you don't want success badly enough, you lazy peasant.

It's aspirational, sure. But it's also complete nonsense. Nobody's life looks like that. What they don't show you is the army of assistants, photographers, and unpaid interns who make that perfection possible. They don't post their 3 a.m. anxiety spirals, their arguments with partners, or their existential dread.

And yet, we buy into it. We convince ourselves that if we could just copy their morning routine, we'd unlock the same level of success. Newsflash: success isn't hiding in your kale smoothie.

Why Nobody Posts Their 3 AM Anxiety Attacks

Here's the thing about the self-help world: it thrives on half-truths and selective storytelling. Nobody posts about the parts of life that don't fit the narrative. The failed business ventures, the sleepless nights, the crushing self-doubt—that's not Instagrammable. Here's what you don't see on their perfectly curated feeds:

* The 47 takes it took to get that "candid" working shot

* The unpaid intern managing their social media

* The credit card debt funding their "luxury lifestyle"

* The relationship problems their "perfect" life is causing

* The existential dread that keeps them posting increasingly desperate content

The real tragedy isn't that they're faking it – it's that we know they're faking it, and we still feel bad about not measuring up to their fictional standards.

The Content Treadmill

The self-help industrial complex operates on a simple principle: Create a problem, sell the solution, create a new problem. Rinse, repeat, profit. It's like a never-ending game of whack-a-mole with your insecurities:

* "You need to hustle!"
* *People burn out*
* "You need work-life balance!"
* *People feel unproductive*
* "You need to hustle mindfully!"
* *People get confused*
* "You need my course on mindful hustling while balancing!"

The Monetization of Misery

Here's the truly insidious part: the industry doesn't just sell solutions — it sells the promise of transformation. And not just any transformation, but the kind that's:

* Quick ("Just 30 days!")
* Easy ("Only 10 minutes a day!")
* Guaranteed ("Or your money back!*")

*Terms and conditions apply, refund requires sacrifice of firstborn child

They're not selling information — most of that's available free on Google. They're selling hope, packaged in a shiny digital course with a fake countdown timer and "limited time" pricing that's been limited for the past three years.

The Great Upsell

Ever notice how no single product is ever enough? There's always:

* The basic course
* The premium course
* The VIP mastermind
* The elite inner circle
* The super-secret platinum level
* The "I can't believe people pay for this" tier

It's like a video game where you never have enough coins to beat the final boss, except the final boss is your own sense of inadequacy, and the coins are very, very real.

Breaking the Cycle

Here's the truth that the self-help industrial complex doesn't want you to realize: You don't need most of what they're selling. In fact, you probably don't need any of it. The most valuable self-help advice could fit on a Post-it note:

* Be kind to yourself
* Do the work
* Get enough sleep
* Move your body
* Drink water
* Don't be a jerk

But try building a six-figure coaching business on that.

The result? A distorted version of reality that makes us feel inadequate. We compare our messy, imperfect lives to their curated highlights and think, "Why can't I get it together?" Meanwhile, they're cashing in on your insecurities.

Conclusion: The Self-Help Scam

The self-help industry isn't about helping you. It's about selling you an image, a fantasy, a promise that life can be as simple and beautiful as an Instagram post. But life isn't simple, and it sure as hell isn't beautiful all the time.

So, the next time you see a "guru" telling you to buy their book or follow their routine, ask yourself: are they helping you, or are they helping themselves? Chances are, it's the latter.

In the next chapter, we'll dissect the anatomy of a charlatan – how they think, how they operate, and why they're so convincingly convincing. Spoiler alert: It involves a lot of buzzwords and strategic hair tousling.

Chapter 3: The Anatomy of a Charlatan

If you're going to spend time studying predators, you might as well start with the apex ones – those perfectly coiffed, perpetually "blessed," professionally whitened-teeth-having merchants of false hope who've turned selling nothing into a multi-million dollar art form.

Red Flags and Red Herrings

Let's get one thing straight: charlatans don't walk around with neon signs that say "CON ARTIST" on their foreheads. They're subtle, charming, and maddeningly convincing. But they do have tells—red flags so obvious you'll kick yourself for missing them once you know what to look for.

Here's a freebie: if someone's solution sounds universal—"This one trick works for everyone!"—run. People are different. What works for a 22-year-old entrepreneur in Bali probably won't work for a 40-year-old single parent juggling three jobs.

Another classic? Overpromising and under-delivering. Charlatans love to dangle impossible outcomes in front of you: "Double your income in 30 days!" or "Guaranteed six-pack abs in two weeks!" But when the dust settles, all you've gained is a lighter wallet and a vague sense of betrayal.

And let's not forget the red herring of "hard work." Charlatans know that scepticism is their biggest enemy, so they pre-empt it by saying, "This isn't a get-rich-quick scheme. It requires effort." That line alone buys them credibility—even if their entire pitch is one giant shortcut.

Let's look at a field guide to spotting charlatans in their natural habitat (usually a rented Airbnb with good lighting). Here are the tell-tale signs:

The Look

* Expensive watch that's always visible in gesturing hands

* A smile that could double as a lighthouse beacon

* "Casual" outfit that costs more than your monthly salary

* Professional photos where they're either:

    o Pointing at a whiteboard

    o Looking pensively into the distance

    o Laughing at their salad

    o Standing next to a car they definitely don't own

The Language

* Uses "quantum" to describe things that have nothing to do with physics

* Sprinkles in "science shows" without ever citing actual studies

* Loves words like "paradigm," "synergy," and "mindset"

* Refers to themselves as a "thought leader," "visionary," or "disruptor"

* Always has a "secret" or "hidden" something they're willing to share (for a price)

The Claims

* "I made $X million using this simple system!"

* "I went from broke to yacht in 6 months!"

* "What I'm about to share will change everything!"

* "The big [industry] doesn't want you to know this!"

If you see these signs, congratulations — you've spotted a charlatan in the wild. Do not approach. Do not make eye contact. Do not give them your email address.

The Confidence Game: Why They're So Damn Convincing

Confidence sells. It's that simple. Charlatans know this, and they wield their self-assurance like a weapon. They don't stutter, hesitate, or leave room for doubt. Their sentences are crisp, their smiles are blinding, and their enthusiasm is infectious.

Here's the psychology: when someone speaks with absolute certainty, we assume they know what they're talking about. It's called the confidence heuristic, and it's why smooth-talking con artists thrive while humble experts often go unnoticed.

But confidence without substance is like a beautifully wrapped box that's empty inside. Charlatans are masters at wrapping their nonsense in just enough jargon to make it sound profound. Throw in a few pseudoscientific buzzwords—"quantum," "synergy," "manifestation"—and suddenly, their nonsense feels legitimate.

The "I Was Just Like You" Story Template

Every charlatan has a backstory. And it always starts the same way: "I was just like you."

They paint a picture of themselves as the underdog—the relatable, struggling everyman or everywoman who overcame insurmountable odds to achieve their current success. The details vary, but the structure is always the same:

1. The Struggle: They were broke, overweight, single, or otherwise miserable.

2. The Discovery: They stumbled upon a "secret" that changed everything.

3. The Transformation: Now they're rich, fit, happily married, and living their best life.

It's a story designed to make you believe two things: (1) They understand your pain because they've been there, and (2) If they can do it, so can you. The first part builds trust; the second part sells the dream.

But here's the kicker: most of these stories are either heavily embellished or outright fabricated. You didn't think they'd let the truth get in the way of a good sales pitch, did you?

It's like a Disney movie, if Disney movies were about selling overpriced online courses.

Here's the template they all use:

"Three years ago, I was [insert relatable struggle]. Then I discovered [insert vague solution] that changed everything. Now I make [insert implausible amount] while sleeping, and I want to help YOU do the same!"

The Mathematical Impossibility of Their Claims

Let's do some quick math on their typical claims:

"I make $100,000 a month passive income!"

* Revenue: $100,000
* Minus taxes: -$30,000
* Minus business expenses: -$20,000
* Minus reality: -$49,999
* Actual income: $1

Secret Ingredient: Just Add Buzzwords

If you want to spot a charlatan in the wild, listen to their language. They love buzzwords. The more meaningless, the better.

Words like "optimization," "biohacking," and "alignment" sound fancy but mean absolutely nothing in most contexts. It's linguistic smoke and mirrors, designed to make you feel like they're operating on a higher intellectual plane.

Charlatans also rely on vague promises that can't be measured or disproven. "Unlock your potential" is a classic. What does that even mean? How do you know when your potential is fully unlocked? Do you get a certificate? A congratulatory email from the universe?

The beauty of these buzzwords is that they're endlessly adaptable. They can be sprinkled onto any pitch, no matter how ridiculous, to give it an air of credibility. They're like human Chat-GPT systems trained exclusively on motivational posters. Here's their secret recipe:

1. Take a basic concept

2. Add unnecessary jargon

3. Make it sound exclusive

4. Throw in some quantum physics

5. Wrap it in a metaphor

6. Price it at $1,997

Example:

* Basic advice: "Set goals and work hard"

* Charlatan version: "Leverage your quantum abundance mindset through my proprietary Neural Success Integration Protocol™ to manifest your destiny in the success frequency!"

The Tactics They Don't Want You to Notice

The False Urgency

"Only 3 spots left!" (Out of an infinite digital product)

"Price goes up in 1:47:26!" (Timer that magically resets)

"Once-in-a-lifetime opportunity!" (Available quarterly)

The Fake Scarcity

* "Limited time offer" (That's been running for three years)
* "Only 100 copies available" (Of a digital product)
* "Exclusive group" (That accepts literally everyone with a pulse and a credit card)

The Social Proof Shell Game

* Testimonials from people who coincidentally all became millionaires
* Screenshots of earnings that are always cropped just so
* Success stories that can't be verified
* Facebook group screenshots showing "amazing results"

Their Greatest Hits of Manipulation

1. The Shame Spiral

    * Make you feel bad about where you are

    * Present their solution as the only way out

    * Shame you for not investing in yourself if you hesitate

2. The False Binary

    * "You can either make excuses or make money!"

    * "There are two types of people: action takers and everyone else!"

    * "You're either growing or dying!"

3. The Investment Flip

* "It's not a cost, it's an investment!"

* "If you think education is expensive, try ignorance!"

* "What's the cost of NOT doing this?"

Why It Works (Even When We Know Better)

The truly insidious part? Even when we know all this, even when we can spot every trick and tactic, their pitches still work on some level. Why? Because they're not really selling courses or systems or secrets. They're selling hope. And hope, as it turns out, is the most addictive substance on Earth.

The Morning After

The worst part isn't falling for their pitch — it's the morning after, when you're looking at your depleted bank account and realizing that their "fool-proof system" is about as fool-proof as a chocolate teapot.

Conclusion: The Charlatan's Playbook

Charlatans thrive on two things: your hope and your ignorance. They know you're desperate for answers, and they're more than happy to exploit that desperation for profit.

The good news? Once you understand their playbook, you'll start seeing through their tricks. Confidence without substance, over-the-top promises, buzzwords galore—it's all there, hiding in plain sight.

The next time someone promises to change your life, ask yourself: Are they selling you a solution, or are they selling you themselves? Because if it's the latter, you're probably looking at a charlatan.

In the next chapter, we'll explore why even the smartest people fall for these obvious scams, and what that says about our wonderfully weird human brains. Spoiler: We're all much more gullible than we think, and that's actually kind of okay.

Chapter 4: The Psychology of Sucker-Proneness

Let's talk about why your brain loves being scammed. Don't take it personally – my brain loves it too. In fact, our brains are basically Yorkshire Terriers chasing after every shiny object that promises to make our lives better, except instead of tennis balls, we're chasing after "revolutionary" productivity apps and detox teas.

Your Brain on Hope

Hope is a hell of a drug. It keeps us going through hard times, pushes us to dream big, and—unfortunately—makes us incredibly easy to scam. Charlatans thrive because we're wired to want hope, even when it's wrapped in a glittery, overpriced package labelled "Ten Steps to Ultimate Success."

Our brains are designed to crave certainty. When life gets messy, unpredictable, or downright terrifying, we latch onto anything that promises stability. A charismatic guru waving a book titled Unlock the Secrets of Life isn't just appealing; they're a lifeboat in a storm. Never mind that the lifeboat is leaking, and they're charging you $299.99 for a paddle.

Hope also blinds us to red flags. When someone dangles the promise of a better future, we're more likely to ignore our instincts and dive in. We want to believe so badly that we don't stop to ask, "Does this make sense?"

Your rational brain knows better. It really does. But then something interesting happens:

The Chemical Cocktail

* Dopamine starts dancing: "Ooh, a solution!"
* Serotonin whispers: "You could be that happy!"
* Cortisol (stress hormone) pipes up: "Better not miss out!"
* Common sense packs its bags and goes on vacation

It's like your brain is hosting a party, and reason wasn't invited.

The Dopamine Hit of "This Is It!"

You know that rush you get when you find a solution that seems perfect? That's dopamine, the brain's way of rewarding you for figuring stuff out—or at least thinking you have. It's the same high you get when you finally solve a puzzle, win a game, or find the perfect meme to send your friend.

Charlatans know how to trigger this response. Their advice is designed to hit you like a bolt of lightning: obvious, profound, and life-changing. "Of course! This is what I've been missing all along!" It's like a mental fireworks show, complete with cheering and confetti.

But here's the problem: dopamine doesn't stick around. Once the high fades, you're left with the same problems you started with. That's why self-help junkies keep coming back for more—they're chasing the next hit of "This is it!"

The Anatomy of an "This Is It!" Moment

Problem Recognition

↓

Anxiety Builds

↓

Solution Appears

↓

Dopamine Explosion

↓

Rational Thinking Temporarily Offline

↓

Credit Card: *exists*

Why Smart People Fall for Dumb Things

If you think you're too smart to be conned, think again. Intelligence doesn't protect you from sucker-proneness—in fact, it might make you more vulnerable. Why? Because smart people are great at rationalizing bad decisions.

"Well, statistically speaking, if only 1% of what they're saying is true, the ROI would still be..."

Stop it, Brian from Accounting. Stop it right now.

Here's how it works:

1. You buy into a scam because it appeals to your emotions (hope, fear, desperation).
2. Your brain realizes something feels off.
3. Instead of admitting you've been duped, you use your intellect to justify your choice.

"This program isn't a scam," you tell yourself. "I just haven't applied it correctly yet." Or, "The advice isn't bad—it just needs more time to work." Sound familiar? That's not logic talking; it's pride.

Smart people also overestimate their ability to spot BS. They think, "I'd never fall for a scam," which makes them less likely to question things. Confidence, meet downfall.

The Amnesia Effect: Why We Forget It Doesn't Work

Ever notice how people keep falling for the same scams over and over again? That's the amnesia effect. Our brains are great at blocking out bad experiences, especially if they make us feel stupid.

Charlatans rely on this. They know that even if their advice doesn't work, you'll forget about it eventually. And when their next book, course, or seminar comes along, you'll think, "This time, it's different."

The amnesia effect is why the same recycled advice keeps popping up in new packaging. It's why fad diets never die, why get-rich–

quick schemes keep evolving, and why self-help books are endlessly rebranded. The cycle continues because we let it.

Conclusion: Understanding Your Inner Sucker

Being sucker-prone doesn't mean you're stupid—it means you're human. We're all wired to hope, to crave certainty, and to chase dopamine. The key is recognizing these tendencies and using them to your advantage instead of letting them be exploited.

When someone promises you the world in ten easy steps, stop and ask yourself: "Am I reacting with my brain or my emotions? Am I thinking this through, or am I just chasing a dopamine hit?"

Remember: the only guaranteed way to stop being a sucker is to start embracing the uncomfortable truth that life is messy, complex, and rarely solvable with a quick fix.

In the next chapter, we'll explore the greatest hits of BS advice – those evergreen nuggets of "wisdom" that sound profound until you think about them for more than three seconds. Spoiler: "Just be yourself" makes the list, right after "Follow your passion all the way to the poorhouse."

Chapter 5: The Greatest Hits of BS Advice

Welcome to the Self-Help Hall of Fame, where vague platitudes go to become Instagram captions. Let's dissect the advice that's been recycled more times than a Hollywood movie plot, each one sold as revolutionary wisdom despite being about as useful as a chocolate teapot.

"Just Be Yourself" (But Not Like That)

Ah, the timeless wisdom of "Just be yourself." Simple, elegant, and entirely useless. What does it even mean? Be the version of yourself that's lazy and binge-watching TV at 2 a.m.? Or the version that overshares at parties and scares away potential friends?

The truth is, "Just be yourself" is advice that only works if you're already the type of person people like. For everyone else, it's a trap. Society doesn't actually want you to be yourself—it wants you to be a curated, polished version that fits its expectations. And heaven forbid you try to figure out what "yourself" actually is. That's a full-time job.

Here's the dirty secret: the people who give this advice rarely follow it. The motivational speaker telling you to embrace your true self? They spent hours crafting their image, practicing their lines, and whitening their teeth. Authenticity is their brand, not their reality.

The Reality Check

Here's the thing: Everyone telling you to "be yourself" is actually selling you a way to be someone else. They're saying:

* "Be yourself... by following my morning routine!"

* "Be yourself... in my signature style!"

* "Be yourself... after buying my personality makeover course!"

It's the ultimate bait-and-switch: They promise authenticity but sell conformity in a beige Instagram filter.

"Follow Your Passion" (And Go Broke)

If we had a dollar for every time someone said, "Follow your passion," we wouldn't need to follow anything because we'd already be rich. This advice sounds wonderful, but it conveniently skips over a critical question: What if your passion doesn't pay the bills?

Nobody tells aspiring poets, interpretive dancers, or professional yo-yo players, "Follow your passion" with a straight face. Why? Because passions are often expensive hobbies, not career paths. And yet, this advice keeps circulating because it feels empowering. It lets us believe that success and happiness are just a passion-pursuit away.

Here's the reality: following your passion is a luxury reserved for people who already have financial stability. For the rest of us, passions are something you juggle alongside your actual responsibilities—like rent, groceries, and the occasional existential crisis.

The truth no one tells you: Most successful people didn't follow their passion – they followed opportunity and became passionate about what worked. Steve Jobs didn't have a burning passion for phone manufacturing. He had a passion for not being broke.

"Think Positive" (While Your House Burns Down)

Positive thinking has become the holy grail of self-help advice. Lost your job? Think positive! Facing a terminal illness? Stay upbeat! House on fire? Well, at least it's a great opportunity to remodel!

Here's the thing: positivity isn't inherently bad. It's useful in moderation, like salt in cooking. But when it becomes the only tool in your mental toolbox, it's downright dangerous. Life is full of situations that suck, and slapping a smiley face on them doesn't make them less awful—it just makes you less prepared to deal with reality.

Charlatans love this advice because it shifts the blame onto you. If their method doesn't work, it's not because their method is garbage—it's because you weren't positive enough. It's a genius scam: they get to take your money and your emotional labour.

The Positive Thinking Pyramid Scheme

Level 1: Think positive

Level 2: Ignore legitimate problems

Level 3: Gaslight yourself about reality

Level 4: Wonder why nothing's changing

Level 5: Buy more positive thinking courses

It's not that positive thinking is bad – it's that it's being sold as a substitute for actual action. It's like trying to fix a flat tire by believing in the inherent roundness of wheels.

"Manifest Your Dreams" (By Buying My Course)

Manifestation is the crown jewel of BS advice. The idea that you can "think" your dreams into existence is as seductive as it is absurd. Want a new car? Just imagine it!

Want a million dollars? Visualize those dollar bills!

It's magical thinking dressed up in modern packaging, and it sells because it lets us believe we're in control of the uncontrollable. The problem? It's utterly divorced from reality.

Manifestation advocates will argue that it works because "you attract what you focus on." But let's be real: focusing on wealth while sitting in your parents' basement doesn't make you wealthy. It makes you a broke person with a vivid imagination.

And let's not ignore the irony: most manifestation gurus make their money by selling you courses, books, and seminars about how to manifest wealth. Their dreams are manifesting, all right—right into their bank accounts.

The Mathematical Probability of Manifestation

Your Thoughts: "I want a million dollars"

Universe: "Cool story, bro"

Probability of Success: Somewhere between zero and LOL

"Rise and Grind" (Until You Collapse)

The hustle culture gurus have turned sleep deprivation into a competitive sport. Their message is clear:

* Sleep is for the weak
* Rest is for the unsuccessful
* Family time is for losers
* If you're not working 25/8, do you even want success?

The Hustle Culture Timeline

5:00 AM – Wake up (post about it)

5:15 AM – Cold shower (post about it)

5:30 AM – Meditate (post about it)

6:00 AM – Work out (post about it)

7:00 AM – Post about posting about hustling

8:00 PM – Collapse from exhaustion

9:00 PM – Post about collapse being part of the journey

The Universal Appeal of Bad Advice

What makes these pieces of advice so popular? Their simplicity. They offer a shortcut—a way to bypass the messy, complicated reality of life. They tell us what we want to hear, not what we need to hear.

"Just be yourself" skips the hard work of self-awareness. "Follow your passion" dodges the uncomfortable truth about financial constraints. "Think positive" ignores the fact that some situations are just bad, no matter how you frame them.

And yet, we keep coming back for more. Why? Because bad advice is like junk food: it's cheap, it's easy, and it feels good in the moment. But in the long run, it leaves us unsatisfied and worse off than before.

The Problem with One-Size-Fits-All Advice

The real issue with all these greatest hits is that they're trying to be universal solutions to specific problems. It's like having one prescription for every medical condition:

Doctor: "Take two 'Follow your passion' and call me in the morning."

Patient: "But my arm is broken."

Doctor: "Sounds like a mindset issue."

Breaking Free from the Platitude Prison

The next time someone tries to sell you repackaged common sense wrapped in a bow of false profundity, remember:

* Generic advice yields generic results
* Real solutions are usually specific and unsexy
* If it fits on a throw pillow, it's probably BS

Conclusion: Spotting the Greatest Hits

The next time someone offers you a one-size-fits-all solution to life's problems, take a step back. Ask yourself: Does this advice actually apply to my situation? Is it actionable, or is it just a platitude? And most importantly, who benefits if I follow it?

Because odds are, the person spouting this advice isn't living by it—they're selling it.

In the next chapter, we'll dive into the Weight Loss Wasteland, where common sense goes to die and your bank account goes to be drained by people selling you the secret to losing weight (Spoiler: It's still diet and exercise, just with better marketing).

Chapter 6: The Weight Loss Wasteland

In the next chapter, we'll dive into the Weight Loss Wasteland, where common sense goes to die and your bank account goes to be drained by people selling you the secret to losing weight (Spoiler: It's still diet and exercise, just with better marketing).

Fifty Years of Fad Diets

Welcome to the eternal merry-go-round of weight loss trends, where every year brings a shiny new promise of instant results. Low-fat, low-carb, high-protein, keto, paleo, carnivore, intermittent fasting—pick your poison. Each fad arrives with the same fervour as a religious movement, only to fade away once the next miracle cure arrives.

But here's the kicker: none of them actually work long-term. Sure, you might lose a few pounds initially, but most people gain it back—and then some. The weight-loss industry knows this. It's built on repeat customers. If their solutions worked, they'd go out of business.

The brilliance of fad diets is their simplicity. "Just cut out all carbs!" "Only eat before noon!" They prey on our desire for quick fixes, ignoring the messy, complex realities of nutrition, exercise, and metabolism. And let's not forget the star endorsements—because if a celebrity swears by it, it must be legit, right?

Let's take a stroll down memory lane, where common sense goes to die and cabbage soup reigns supreme:

The 1970s

* The Grapefruit Diet (Because scurvy is slimming)

* The Sleeping Beauty Diet (Can't eat if you're sedated!)

* The Cookie Diet (Finally, a religion we can believe in)

The 1980s

* The Beverly Hills Diet (For when you hate both money and joy)

* The Cabbage Soup Diet (Turn your body into a biological weapon)

* The Liquid Diet (Chewing is so last decade)

The 1990s

* The Blood Type Diet (Science fiction meets nutrition)

* The Zone Diet (Math homework with meals)

* The Raw Food Diet (For people who hate microwaves and happiness)

The 2000s

* The South Beach Diet (Because geographical locations make you thin)
* The Master Cleanse (Spicy lemonade will save us all)
* Atkins 2.0 (Now with more bacon!)

The 2010s

* Keto (Atkins in a party dress)
* Intermittent Fasting (Skipping breakfast, but make it science)
* Clean Eating (Regular food, but more expensive)

The 2020s

* Digital Fasting (Like regular fasting, but with an app)
* AI-Powered Meal Planning (A robot tells you to eat vegetables)

* Gut Health Protocol (Everyone's a microbiologist now)

The Before-and-After Photo Scam

Ah, the magical before-and-after photo—the weight-loss industry's favourite bait. On the left: a sad, slouching person with bad lighting. On the right: the same person, smiling, standing tall, and bathed in golden light. It's marketing genius.

But let's break it down. These photos are riddled with manipulation. The "before" shot is deliberately unflattering, with poor posture, baggy clothes, and zero effort. The "after" shot, meanwhile, gets the royal treatment: good lighting, a flattering outfit, and maybe even a touch of Photoshop.

And here's the dirty little secret: sometimes the order of the photos is reversed. Fitness models are hired to "gain weight" for the "before" shot, then return to their usual physique for the "after." It's smoke and mirrors, designed to make you think, "If they can do it, so can I!" Spoiler: you can't, because they didn't.

Why Every Month Is "Bikini Body" Month

The weight-loss industry has perfected the art of making you feel inadequate. January is for "New Year, New You!" April is for "Get Ready for Summer!" Fall? "Slim Down Before the Holidays!" And December? "Undo the Holiday Damage!"

The message is clear: you're never good enough. There's always a new reason to feel bad about your body and a new product to fix it. This cycle of guilt and aspiration is what keeps the industry afloat.

But let's talk about the term "bikini body" for a second. It's a loaded phrase that implies your body is only valid if it meets some arbitrary standard. Newsflash: if you have a body and a bikini, you already have a bikini body. The problem isn't your body; it's the billion-dollar industry telling you otherwise.

The Mathematics of Impossible Promises

"Lose 10 pounds in a week!" "Drop 30 pounds in 30 days!" These promises sound amazing, but they defy the laws of biology. Sustainable weight loss happens slowly— about 1-2 pounds per week for most people. Anything faster is usually water weight, muscle loss, or, worse, a sign that you're starving yourself.

Charlatans love to throw around numbers because they sound scientific. But when you dig deeper, the math doesn't add up. A pound of fat equals about 3,500 calories. To lose 10 pounds in a week, you'd need to create a deficit of 35,000 calories—or 5,000 per day. Unless you're running ultramarathons while fasting, that's not happening.

These promises aren't just unrealistic; they're harmful. They set people up for failure, erode self-esteem, and perpetuate the myth that weight loss is a quick and easy process. It's not. It's hard, messy, and deeply personal.

Conclusion: Breaking Free from the Weight-Loss Wasteland

The weight-loss industry thrives on your insecurities, your desperation, and your hope. It sells you shortcuts that don't work and blames you when you fail. The truth is, there's no magic diet, no secret exercise, no "one weird trick" that will solve everything.

If you're serious about improving your health, skip the fads and focus on the basics: balanced nutrition, regular movement, and a mindset rooted in self-compassion, not self-loathing. It's not sexy, and it won't sell millions of books, but it's the only advice that actually works.

And remember: your worth isn't tied to a number on a scale or a dress size. You don't need to buy what they're selling, because you're already enough.

Chapter 7: The Get-Rich-Quick Cemetery

Welcome to the final resting place of countless get-rich-quick schemes, where dreams of passive income go to die and cryptocurrency whitepapers decompose in digital graves. Let's take a tour through the memorial gardens of failed financial fantasies.

Graveyards of Failed "Fool-proof" Systems

Every few years, a new "fool-proof" way to get rich emerges, promising wealth beyond your wildest dreams with minimal effort. From flipping houses to flipping NFTs, the systems might change, but the pitch remains the same: "Act now, and you'll never have to work another day in your life!"

The truth? These systems are fool-proof only in the sense that fools are always proof they work—for the people selling them. The graveyards are full of failed schemes, each with a trail of empty wallets, shattered dreams, and regretful late-night Google searches.

Here's the pattern: someone claims they've unlocked the secret to financial freedom, sells you their "proven" system, and disappears when the lawsuits start piling up. Their success doesn't come from the system—it comes from selling the system to suckers.

Crypto Bros and Digital Snake Oil

Cryptocurrency promised to democratize wealth and upend the traditional financial system. Instead, it created a gold rush for scammers, opportunists, and tech-savvy snake oil salesmen.

Enter the Crypto Bro: a guy in a rented Lamborghini, flashing screenshots of his Bitcoin gains and promising you, "It's not too late to get in!" Spoiler alert: it's always too late to get in. By the time you hear about the next big crypto opportunity, the real money has already been made—by the people selling it to you.

Crypto scams thrive on FOMO (fear of missing out). They dangle the promise of astronomical returns, convincing you to invest before you understand what you're buying. And when it all crashes? The Crypto Bros are long gone, sipping margaritas paid for by your life savings.

The "Passive Income" Paradox

"Make money while you sleep!" It's the dream of passive income, sold to you by people who are very much awake, actively working to take your money. From drop shipping to affiliate marketing to renting out imaginary properties in the metaverse, the promise is the same: endless cash flow with zero effort.

Here's the paradox: creating truly passive income is hard, often requiring years of active work, upfront investment, and a bit of luck. Even then, it's not guaranteed. The people making real passive income? They're usually the ones selling you the dream—not living it.

Consider this: if someone had a fool-proof way to make money passively, why would they share it with you? Wouldn't they just quietly rake in the cash? The answer is obvious—they're selling you the dream because that's their passive income stream.

Why Nobody Sells Their Money-Making Secrets

Think about it: if you'd discovered a guaranteed way to make millions, would you tell everyone about it? Of course not. You'd keep it to yourself and quietly enjoy your fortune. The very act of selling money-making secrets should be a red flag.

The gurus peddling these secrets aren't wealthy because they cracked some magical code. They're wealthy because they convinced you to pay $997 for their webinar. They're not teachers; they're salespeople.

These schemes rely on a simple formula:

1. Create a sense of exclusivity. ("This opportunity isn't for everyone!")

2. Play on your insecurities. ("Are you tired of working a dead-end job?")

3. Offer a solution that feels attainable but vague. ("I'll show you how to make six figures from home!")

4. Take your money and run.

The Cycle of Get-Rich-Quick Desperation

The get-rich-quick cemetery exists because people are desperate. They want an escape from debt, dead-end jobs, and financial stress. Charlatans exploit that desperation, offering hope in the form of half-baked systems and hollow promises.

And when one scheme fails, people don't give up—they move on to the next one, convinced that this time will be different. It's a vicious cycle, fuelled by FOMO, insecurity, and the human desire for an easier life.

Think Twice

The Million-Dollar Question:

If someone has discovered a fool-proof way to make millions, why would they:

1. Stop doing it to teach others?

2. Share it with competitors?

3. Sell it for $47?

The Course Creator's Dilemma:

If (moneyMakingSystem == true) {

return keepSecretAndGetRich();

} else {

return sellCoursesAboutGettingRich();

}

The Economics of Empty Promises

Let's break down the real numbers behind these opportunities:

Investment Required:

* Course: $1,997

* "Essential" Tools: $499/month

* "Optional" Coaching: $5,000

* Your Dignity: Priceless

Return on Investment:

* Financial: Negative

* Educational: Learning what not to do

* Psychological: Trust issues

* Social: Fewer friends after attempting to recruit them

The Red Flags Anthology

Course Sales Pages:

* Countdown timers that never end
* Screenshots of bank accounts
* Lamborghinis in thumbnails
* "Value" of $9,997 marked down to $47
* Testimonials from "John S." and "Mary P."

Common Promises:

* "Financial freedom in 30 days!"
* "Never work again!"
* "Secret system banks don't want you to know!"
* "Turn $100 into $10,000!"
* "No experience needed!"

Translation: "No experience preferred, critical thinking discouraged"

The True Cost of Getting Rich Quick

Financial Cost:

* Money invested
* Money lost
* Money spent on recovery
* Money needed for therapy

Personal Cost:

* Time wasted
* Relationships strained
* LinkedIn connections lost
* Facebook friends muted

Breaking Free from the Cycle

The truth about getting rich:

1. It's usually boring
2. It takes time
3. There are no secrets
4. If it sounds too good to be true, it is
5. The only people getting rich quick are selling courses about getting rich quick

The Final Resting Place

Here's what you'll find in every failed get-rich-quick scheme:

* Empty promises
* Complicated systems
* "Proprietary" methods

* Your money

Conclusion: The Real Path to Wealth

Here's the inconvenient truth: building wealth takes time, effort, and discipline. There are no shortcuts, no magic formulas, no "one weird trick." The real path to financial stability isn't sexy—it's boring. Save money. Invest wisely. Learn skills that are in demand.

Charlatans won't tell you this because it doesn't sell. But the sooner you embrace the reality of slow, steady progress, the sooner you can stop throwing your money into the get-rich-quick cemetery.

And remember: the only person getting rich off these schemes is the one selling them. Don't be their next victim.

In the next chapter, we'll explore the Relationship Racket, where dating coaches and pickup artists promise to solve your love life with the same level of success as a chocolate teapot in a sauna.

Chapter 8: The Relationship Racket

Welcome to the industry that's managed to monetize human connection, where love comes with a price tag and relationships are reduced to algorithms. It's time to explore the wonderful world of people who think they can fix your love life for five easy payments of $99.99.

Finding Love in Five Easy Payments

In the world of dating advice, love isn't just in the air—it's on sale. From "Find Your Soulmate in 30 Days" courses to $10,000 matchmaking services, the relationship racket thrives on selling one thing: the idea that you're fundamentally broken and need expert help to find love.

And let's not ignore the sheer absurdity of it all. One "dating guru" will tell you to play hard to get; another will insist you need to be open and vulnerable. One course says men love the chase; another claims they want emotional security. It's like trying to solve a Rubik's Cube where the colours keep changing.

The truth? Relationships are messy, unpredictable, and deeply personal. There's no five-step formula for love—unless you're in love with losing money.

What They Promise vs. What You Get

What They Promise	What You Get
Soulmate in 30 days	30 days of awkward coffee dates
Perfect relationship	New insecurities

Dating "secrets"	Common sense in a PDF
Lifetime happiness	Subscription renewal notice
Expert guidance	Google results in fancy font

The Dating Coach Disaster

Dating coaches love to present themselves as experts, but their qualifications are usually as flimsy as their advice. Many of them are self-appointed authorities with no formal training, no relevant education, and no track record beyond "I once had a girlfriend."

Their advice often boils down to rehashed clichés dressed up as revolutionary insights. "Be confident!" "Put yourself out there!" "Don't settle!" These are things your grandmother could tell you—for free. But instead, you're paying someone hundreds (or thousands) of dollars to hear it in a PowerPoint presentation.

The worst part? Some of these so-called coaches actively promote toxic behaviour, encouraging manipulation, dishonesty, or downright creepy tactics. If your dating strategy involves "negging" someone into liking you, you might want to rethink both your approach and your humanity.

Why All Relationship Advice Contradicts Itself

Ever notice how every piece of relationship advice seems to contradict the one before it? Be yourself, but also reinvent yourself. Be independent, but also make them feel needed. Communicate openly, but also maintain an air of mystery.

This isn't a coincidence—it's a feature of the relationship racket. By giving you conflicting advice, charlatans ensure that no matter what happens, they can claim they were right. If you follow their advice and it works, they're geniuses. If it doesn't, you "misunderstood" or "didn't apply it properly." Heads they win, tails you lose.

The reality is that relationships are too complex to distil into simple rules. They're shaped by individual personalities, circumstances, and timing—none of which can be predicted by a one-size-fits-all formula.

The Marriage Manual Mayhem

Marriage advice is a racket within a racket. Entire industries are built around convincing couples that their relationship is doomed unless they buy a specific book, attend a specific retreat, or follow a specific guru.

These so-called experts often peddle advice that's as obvious as it is unhelpful. "Communicate more." "Spend quality time together." "Appreciate each other." Gee, thanks, Captain Obvious. What's next? "Breathe regularly and don't forget to eat"?

Meanwhile, the advice that actually works—like therapy, honest conversations, and hard work—is rarely marketed as a quick fix. That's because it's difficult, time-consuming, and doesn't come with a snazzy tagline.

The Relationship Racket's Ultimate Con

What makes the relationship industry so successful is its ability to prey on insecurity. If you're single, they'll convince you it's because you're doing something wrong. If you're in a relationship, they'll convince you it's not good enough. If you're married, they'll convince you it's on the brink of collapse unless you buy their course, book, or seminar.

And here's the kicker: even if their advice doesn't work, you'll rarely blame them. Instead, you'll blame yourself. "Maybe I wasn't confident enough." "Maybe I didn't try hard enough." It's a perfect scam, designed to keep you coming back for more.

Conclusion: Love Is Not for Sale

Here's the truth no one wants to admit: there's no shortcut to love. There's no magic formula, no guaranteed method, no foolproof system. Love is messy, unpredictable, and often inconvenient. It doesn't follow rules, and it certainly doesn't come with a money-back guarantee.

The next time someone tries to sell you the secret to finding or keeping love, ask yourself this: if their method worked, why are they spending their time selling advice instead of living their perfect love story?

Because odds are, they're not experts—they're salespeople. And love, real love, can't be bought.

In the next chapter, we'll face the ultimate uncomfortable truth: why quick fixes don't fix anything, and why that's actually good news for those willing to do the real work.

Chapter 9: Breaking Free from the BS

Welcome to your deprogramming session. By now, you've seen the circus of charlatans, the parade of promises, and the endless echo chamber of expensive empty advice. It's time to develop your immunity to industrial-grade BS. Consider this your vaccination against viral stupidity.

Developing Your Bull** Detector**

Congratulations! If you've made it this far, your tolerance for BS is likely at an all-time low. You're now primed to develop one of the most valuable skills in modern life: the ability to detect bull**** before it gets its sticky little hooks into your wallet, brain, or self-esteem.

Step one: adopt the mantra "This sounds too good to be true" and repeat it until it becomes a reflex. If a product, person, or system promises instant results, endless happiness, or guaranteed success, your first instinct should be suspicion. Quick fixes are rarely fixes, and guarantees are usually hollow.

Step two: learn to follow the money. Who benefits from you believing this? Are they selling something? Are they relying on your desperation, insecurity, or lack of information? Most BS doesn't survive even a cursory inspection of the profit motive behind it.

Step three: embrace scepticism as a lifestyle. Scepticism doesn't mean you reject everything—it means you question everything. It means you ask hard questions, demand evidence, and aren't afraid to walk away when the answers don't add up.

The BS Detection Checklist:

1. The Promise Check

If it sounds too good to be true...

*   It is
*   It really is
*   Seriously, stop looking for loopholes
*   It. Just. Is.

2. The Urgency Test

*   Is there a countdown timer?
*   Is it a "limited time offer"?
*   Will the price "go up soon"?
*   Is there artificial scarcity?

If yes to any of these, your BS detector should be screaming louder than a car alarm at 3 AM.

3. The Credential Inspection

When they say	Ask yourself
"Self-made millionaire"	Why are they selling $47 courses?
"Expert in the field"	According to whom?
"Guru"	Why not an actual job title?
"School of life"	So... no real credentials?
"Results may vary"	You mean... won't happen?

The Power of "This Sounds Too Good"

"This sounds too good to be true" is the most underrated survival skill of our time. It's the mental speed bump that stops you from buying miracle weight-loss tea, signing up for a "guaranteed" business opportunity, or believing that influencer's "completely organic" skincare routine.

The beauty of this phrase is that it works everywhere. A 15-minute morning routine that promises to make you a millionaire? Sounds too good. A diet that lets you eat unlimited bacon while losing weight? Definitely too good. A self-help book that promises to change your life in one weekend? Run.

Embracing the Messy Truth

Here's the uncomfortable reality: life is complicated, solutions are rarely simple, and real progress takes time. The messy truth isn't sexy or marketable, but it's the only thing that actually works.

Want to get in shape? It's going to require consistent effort, not a magic supplement.

Want to find love? You'll have to embrace the vulnerability and unpredictability of real human connection, not rely on a "how-to" guide. Want to build wealth? It's going to take hard work, smart decisions, and years of patience, not a get-rich-quick scheme.

Why Real Solutions Never Fit on a Post-It Note

Charlatans love bite-sized wisdom because it feels digestible and actionable. But real solutions? They don't fit on Post-It Notes, Instagram captions, or Tik-Tok videos. They're nuanced, complex, and often require context, effort, and introspection.

Take the classic "Think positive!" advice. Sure, maintaining a good attitude helps, but it's not a solution. If you're drowning in debt, positive thinking alone won't save you. If you're in a toxic relationship, no amount of optimism will magically fix the other person. Real solutions involve actionable steps, not platitudes.

The Courage to Call BS

Calling out BS isn't always easy. It requires courage to stand against the crowd, especially when the crowd is busy applauding the latest guru, trend, or fad. But the more you practice, the better you'll get at it—and the freer you'll feel.

It's liberating to realize you don't have to buy into the hype, the quick fixes, or the magical thinking. You can step back, evaluate, and say, "No thanks." And when you do, you'll find yourself saving time, money, and sanity.

The BS-Free Decision Making Framework

When evaluating any claim, product, or service:

The Five Questions:
1. What's the worst that could happen?
2. What's the most likely outcome?
3. What's the opportunity cost?
4. What are the alternatives?
5. What happens if I do nothing?

The Reality Filter:

Incoming Claim

↓

Is it too good to be true?

↓

Yes → Reject

No → Continue

↓

Is there evidence?

↓

Yes → Verify

No → Reject

↓

Is it selling hope?

↓

Yes → Be sceptical

No → Consider carefully

Building Long-Term Immunity

Remember these eternal truths:

1. If it's revolutionary, it probably isn't
2. If it's a secret, it's probably common knowledge
3. If it's urgent, it's probably manipulative
4. If it's guaranteed, read the fine print

5. If it's easy, it's probably ineffective

The Vaccination Schedule:
- Daily: Question one assumption
- Weekly: Research one claim
- Monthly: Review your beliefs
- Yearly: Audit your subscriptions

The Path Forward

Breaking free from BS doesn't mean becoming cynical. It means:

- Being realistically optimistic
- Accepting complexity
- Embracing uncertainty
- Valuing evidence
- Respecting process

* Understanding nuance

Conclusion: Welcome to the Anti-BS Club

Breaking free from BS doesn't mean you'll never be fooled again. It just means you'll be fooled less often and for shorter periods. You'll learn to see the patterns, spot the red flags, and trust your instincts.

Life is messy, unpredictable, and full of challenges. There are no shortcuts, but there is power in embracing the journey for what it is: imperfect, difficult, and uniquely yours.

So welcome to the anti-BS club. There are no secret handshakes, no 10-step plans, and definitely no membership fees. Just a shared commitment to cutting through the noise and living a life that's honest, real, and a little bit messier—but a whole lot more satisfying.

In the next chapter, we'll face the ultimate uncomfortable truth: why quick fixes don't fix anything, and why that's actually good news for those willing to do the real work.

Chapter 10: The Uncomfortable Truth

Look, we need to talk. And by "talk," I mean I'm about to serve you a triple-shot espresso of reality that's going to make that $7 motivational green juice you bought this morning taste like broken dreams and empty promises.

Why Quick Fixes Don't Fix Anything

Let's rip the Band-Aid off: quick fixes don't work. Not in weight loss, not in relationships, not in wealth-building, and certainly not in personal growth. Why? Because life isn't a flat tire you can patch up and forget about. It's more like a decades-long hike through unpredictable terrain—messy, exhausting, and occasionally full of bear attacks.

Quick fixes appeal to us because they promise to make the hike easier. They offer shortcuts, cheat codes, and the illusion that you can bypass the hard stuff. But every shortcut ends the same way: you circle back to the beginning, usually with less money and more frustration than when you started.

The uncomfortable truth is that lasting change requires time, effort, and discomfort. It's not glamorous, and it doesn't sell well, but it's the only path that works.

Remember that time you downloaded that meditation app that promised inner peace in just 10 minutes a day? How's that working out for you? Still feeling like a zen master while screaming at your Wi-Fi router? Yeah, thought so.

The problem isn't that quick fixes don't work at all – it's that they work just enough to keep us hooked. They're the equivalent of eating one potato chip. It satisfies you for approximately 2.7 seconds before you're elbow-deep in the bag, wondering where it all went wrong.

The Beauty of Slow, Painful Progress

If quick fixes are junk food for the soul, slow progress is a home-cooked meal. It's not flashy or instant, but it's nourishing and sustainable. Slow progress forces you to confront your habits, assumptions, and fears. It's not about hacking your way to success; it's about building a foundation that doesn't crumble under pressure.

But here's the real kicker: that boring stuff? It's actually beautiful in its own twisted way. It's beautiful because it's real. It's beautiful because it's yours. And most importantly, it's beautiful because unlike that "Manifest Your Dream Life in 24 Hours" workshop you attended, it actually fucking works.

Think about anything truly worthwhile in your life. Did it come easy? Probably not. Your achievements, relationships, and personal growth likely came from effort, patience, and learning from failure. That's the beauty of slow progress—it's hard-earned and deeply satisfying.

But here's the real kicker: that boring stuff? It's actually beautiful in its own twisted way. It's beautiful because it's real. It's beautiful because it's yours. And most importantly, it's beautiful because unlike that "Manifest Your Dream Life in 24 Hours" workshop you attended, it actually fucking works.

Let's break down what real progress looks like:

* It's the kind of progress that makes you want to quit at least twice a week

* It's showing up when your motivation has left the building and is halfway to Mexico

* It's failing so many times that you start to think failure is your new hobby

It's celebrating improvements so small that trying to explain them to anyone else makes you sound insane

Learning to Love the Journey (Even When It Sucks)

The self-help industry loves to talk about "loving the journey," but they usually mean it in a shallow, Instagrammable way. Real journeys are rarely pretty. They're full of setbacks, self-doubt, and days when you want to give up.

The secret isn't learning to love the suck – it's learning to high-five yourself for dealing with the suck anyway. It's about building a relationship with discomfort that doesn't involve immediately reaching for your phone and googling "how to never feel uncomfortable again."

Think of it like this: if personal growth were a movie, the montage would be about 3 minutes long. Reality is the other 23 hours and 57 minutes of the day where you're just trying to figure out which end is up.

Loving the journey doesn't mean enjoying every moment. It means accepting that the hard parts are just as important as the victories. It means understanding that failure is a feature, not a bug. It means finding meaning in the process, not just the outcome.

And yes, it sucks sometimes. But the alternative—chasing one quick fix after another—is even worse.

Why This Book Won't Change Your Life (And That's OK)

Let's be honest: this book isn't going to change your life. It's not a magical blueprint, a fool-proof system, or a 10-step plan to eternal happiness. It's just a guide—a flashlight to help you see through the fog of BS. No book will. Books don't change lives – people change their own lives, usually through a messy combination of:

* Repeated failure

* Stubborn persistence

* Blind luck

* More failure

* That one moment where everything clicks (followed by more failure)

If you're looking for a guarantee, here's the only one I can offer: everything worth doing is going to take longer than you want, be harder than you expected, and involve more embarrassing moments than you're prepared for.

Life isn't meant to be changed by a single book, course, or seminar. It's meant to be shaped by the small, consistent actions you take every day. This book's job isn't to transform you—it's to remind you that transformation is a long, messy process that only you can navigate.

Here's the good news: once you accept that there are no shortcuts, you can stop wasting time looking for them. You can stop beating yourself up for not transforming your entire existence through a weekend workshop. You can stop wondering why everyone else seems to have figured it all out (spoiler alert: they haven't).

Instead, you can get down to the real work of changing your life: showing up, doing the thing, screwing up, learning from it, and doing it again. And again. And again.

Is it sexy? Hell no.

Is it marketable? About as marketable as a chocolate teapot.

Does it work? Slowly, painfully, and more reliably than any five-step solution you'll ever buy.

And if that's not enough for you, I hear there's a great seminar next weekend about manifesting your best life through the power of positive thinking and crystal-infused water. Only $999! (Results not guaranteed, void where prohibited, please don't sue me.)

Conclusion: Now What?

So here we are, at the end of this anti-self-help journey. If you're waiting for the part where I reveal the secret sauce, the magic formula, or the hidden path to enlightenment – well, you clearly haven't been paying attention. But since you've made it this far, let's talk about what you can actually do with all this newfound cynicism.

Here's the real secret: the moment you let go of the quest for quick fixes, you gain something far more valuable—freedom. Freedom to embrace imperfection. Freedom to make mistakes. Freedom to stop chasing someone else's idea of success and start defining your own.

Letting go of BS doesn't mean you'll never be tempted by it again. You will. We all are. But every time you choose the messy, honest truth over the shiny, hollow promise, you get a little stronger.

So here's to the slow, painful, beautiful journey. It won't be easy, but it will be worth it.

The Anti-Self-Help Action Plan

First things first: throw out your vision board. I'm kidding – keep it if you want, but maybe add some realistic photos to balance out those Maldives beach shots. Like maybe a picture of you doing your taxes, or dealing with a passive-aggressive email from your boss.

Here's your actual action plan:

1. Stop looking for action plans. Seriously. Life doesn't come with an IKEA instruction manual, and if it did, you'd still end up with extra pieces and wondering if that wobbly bit is going to collapse at 3 AM.

2. Start keeping a "BS Journal." Every time you catch yourself falling for some too-good-to-be-true promise, write it down. Not to shame yourself,

but to start noticing your own patterns. Are you particularly vulnerable to anything promising "financial freedom" after watching your bank account on a Sunday night? Do you stockpile productivity apps every time you miss a deadline? Knowing your BS triggers is half the battle.

3. Embrace the power of "probably not." The next time someone promises you overnight success, automatic weight loss, or instant happiness, just say "probably not" and move on with your day. It's surprisingly liberating.

Building BS Immunity

Think of BS immunity like building actual immunity – you're going to have to expose yourself to some germs. In this case, the germs are your own mistakes, failures, and occasional lapses in judgment. Every time you fall for something and realize it later, you're actually getting stronger. You're developing antibodies against nonsense.

Here's what BS immunity looks like in practice:

* You see a "guaranteed 6-figure business blueprint" and actually laugh out loud

* You don't feel the need to try every new diet that promises to "revolutionize your relationship with food"

* You can watch motivational videos without immediately buying the speaker's course

* You understand that adding "quantum" to anything doesn't make it more scientific

* You've accepted that your morning routine doesn't need to start at 4 AM to be valid

Why You'll Probably Still Fall for Something

Let's be real: even after reading this book, you're probably going to fall for something else. Maybe not today, maybe not tomorrow, but someday, when you're tired, or stressed, or particularly vulnerable, some snake oil salesman is going to catch you at the right moment with the right pitch.

And you know what? That's okay.

Being BS-proof isn't about never falling for anything – it's about falling less often, catching yourself faster, and recovering more quickly. It's about building resilience, not perfection.

Think of it like this: you're going to get sick sometimes, even if you eat all your vegetables and take your vitamins. The goal isn't to never get sick; it's to have a strong enough immune system to bounce back quickly. The same goes for your BS detector.

A Final Note on Hope (The Real Kind)

Here's the thing about hope: the real kind isn't sexy. It doesn't come with a money-back guarantee or a five-step implementation plan. Real hope is messy, persistent, and often looks a lot like stubbornness.

Real hope is:

* Showing up even when the motivation influencers are quiet
* Starting over for the hundredth time without posting about it
* Doing the work without needing to call yourself a "warrior" or "goddess"
* Understanding that progress often looks like maintenance

The truth is, you don't need another self-help book after this one. You don't need another course, seminar, or mastermind group. What you need is already within you – not in some woo-woo "unlock your inner potential" way, but in a "you already know what to do, you're just looking for excuses not to do it" way.

So here's my final prescription (which you should absolutely not take as medical advice):

* Take one dose of reality every morning

* Mix it with a healthy spoonful of self-compassion

* Add a dash of stubborn determination

* And chase it with the understanding that if something sounds too good to be true, it's probably being sold by someone with a course to pitch

Remember: the next time you're tempted by a miracle solution, ask yourself: "What would that cynical book say about this?" And then maybe, just maybe, save your money for something more useful – like therapy, or pizza, or both. Because sometimes the most revolutionary act is simply admitting that revolution doesn't come in a ten-step program.

And if all else fails, remember this: the gurus selling happiness probably aren't as happy as their Instagram feeds suggest. But you? You're doing just fine, messy progress and all.

Now go forth and be sceptical. But not too sceptical. Just sceptical enough to keep your wallet in your pants and your BS detector on medium-high.

The End.

(No upsells, no hidden chapters, no secret bonus content available for just three easy payments. Just the end. Really.)

Appendix A: The BS Bingo Card

Ladies and gentlemen, print this out, grab your markers, and join us for everyone's favourite game show: "How Many BS Buzzwords Can You Spot Before Your Brain Melts?" Score five in a row, and you win the grand prize of keeping your money in your wallet!

Common Phrases That Should Make You Run

▶ "This isn't a get-rich-quick scheme..." (Narrator: It was.)

Charlatans have a knack for using phrases that sound profound but are essentially meaningless. Consider this your cheat sheet for spotting their nonsense.

"Unlock your true potential!" Translation: Pay me to tell you things you already know.

"This one weird trick..." Translation: Prepare to be scammed.

"Experts don't want you to know this!" Translation: No actual expert would endorse this.

"Just follow these simple steps!" Translation: This will oversimplify your problem and leave you frustrated.

"Guaranteed results!" Translation: Results not actually guaranteed.

The Ultimate Charlatan Checklist

Think you've encountered a guru, influencer, or self-help saviour? Use this checklist to find out:

1. Do they promise quick, effortless results?

2. Are they selling a course, product, or coaching package?

3. Do they heavily use buzzwords like manifestation, alignment, grind, hack?

4. Do they claim to have cracked a secret no one else knows?

5. Do they use testimonials instead of evidence?

6. Are they more famous for being an expert than actually doing anything?

If you answered "yes" to three or more, congratulations—you've spotted a charlatan!

The "Trust Me, I'm Special" Collection:

* "What your doctor doesn't want you to know..."

* "The secret that [industry] doesn't want you to discover..."

* "Unlike other [experts/coaches/gurus]..."

* "They called me crazy, but..."

* "What I'm about to share will shock you..."

The "Time Is Running Out" Greatest Hits:

* "Limited time offer" (that's been running since 2019)

* "Only X spots left!" (in an automated webinar)

* "Price goes up at midnight!" (in every time zone)

* "Once-in-a-lifetime opportunity" (available monthly)

* "Bonus expires in [suspiciously specific time]"

The "Magic Numbers" Series:

* "The 3 secrets to..." (Why is it always 3?)

* "10X your..." (Why not 11X? Too specific?)

* "7-figure" (Because 6 figures is for peasants)

* "Triple your results in 30 days"

* "2-minute hack that will..." (It won't.)

The "Quantum Nonsense" Collection:

* "Quantum healing"
* "Vibrational alignment"
* "Energy frequencies"
* "DNA activation"
* "Cellular reprogramming" (Your cells are fine, Karen.)

Red Flag Dictionary

Buzzword Overload: When every sentence feels like it was written by a motivational poster generator.

Vague Timelines: Promises like "See results in as little as 30 days!" with no mention of what happens if you don't.

Lifestyle Flexing: Flashy cars, private jets, and beachfront selfies that scream, "This could be you!" Spoiler: it won't.

Excessive Testimonials: When they drown you in "success stories" but never explain how it actually works.

Appendix B: The Wall of Shame

Greatest Hits of Terrible Advice

Here's a curated collection of some of the worst advice to ever grace a book, seminar, or viral social media post:

1. "Just be yourself!"—Unless yourself is an anxious wreck, in which case, don't.

2. "Wake up at 5 AM to be successful!"—Because sleep deprivation is the secret to happiness.

3. "Follow your passion!"—But only if your passion is financially viable, which most aren't.

4. "Think positive!"—Sure, because optimism alone will pay the bills.

Failed Predictions and Promises:

2015:

* "Email is dead!"

* Status: Email is still very much alive and judging you for not responding

* Predicted by: Every social media guru trying to sell their DM course

2018:

* "Bitcoin will hit $1 million by 2020!"

* Status: *awkward coughing*

* Predicted by: Every crypto bro with a YouTube channel

2020:

- * "Traditional education is over!"
- * Status: Students still studying, just with worse posture
- * Predicted by: Online course creators, surprisingly

2022:

- * "AI will replace all jobs by 2023!"
- * Status: AI mostly writing dad jokes and arguing on Twitter
- * Predicted by: People selling AI courses

Where Are They Now? (Spoiler: Selling Something New)

Many charlatans have an incredible ability to rebrand. When their weight-loss program fails, they pivot to mindfulness coaching. When their get-rich-quick scheme collapses, they suddenly become "experts" in personal resilience.

The Transformation Timeline:

1. Fitness Guru → Mindset Coach → Crypto Expert → AI Consultant → "Holistic Wellness Integration Specialist" (Still nobody knows what this means)

The Eternal Pivot Masters:

Dave "Get Rich Quick" Johnson

* 2020: Forex trading expert
* 2021: NFT consultant
* 2022: Mindset coach
* 2023: AI prompt engineer
* 2024: Time travel consultant (probably)

Sarah "Living Your Best Life" Smith

* Started: Selling fitness tea

* Moved to: Selling fitness courses
* Pivoted to: Selling course-creation courses
* Currently: Selling courses about selling courses about selling courses
* Next year: Quantum blockchain mindset coaching (taking bets)

The Eternal Constants:

* That one guy still selling the same webinar from 2016
* The "mindset coach" who changes niches every 3 months
* The "business guru" who's never run a business besides teaching business
* The "lifestyle expert" living with their parents
* The "seven-figure consultant" who counts the decimal places

Special Recognition Awards:

🏆 The "Most Creative Use of the Word 'Quantum'" Award

🏆 The "Most Pyramid Schemes Disguised as Network Marketing" Award

🏆 The "Most Ridiculous Income Claims in a Single Post" Award

🏆 The "Most Stock Photos Used in 'Personal' Success Story" Award

🏆 Lifetime Achievement Award for Consistent Pivoting

Remember: This wall of shame is a living document. As long as there are dreams to crush and wallets to empty, there will be bold innovators finding new ways to separate people from their money while adding the word "quantum" to random business proposals.

(Note: Names have been changed to protect the guilty, but let's be honest – they'll probably try to sell you something anyway.)

About Author

Mwape Kalembwe is a renowned mathematician and data analyst. He lives in Zambia.

Credits

Front cover design: @hellomuh22 | Freepik

Copyright

Copyright © 2025 by Mwape Kalembwe. All rights reserved under international copyright laws. Upon payment of the necessary fees, you are granted a nonexclusive, non-transferable right to view and read this e-book on-screen. Reproduction, transmission, downloading, decompiling, reverse-engineering, or storage of any part of this text in any format or by any means, whether electronic or mechanical, is prohibited without the express written consent of Such Academy.

Printed in Dunstable, United Kingdom